The Rules for Dogs

Other Books by Leigh Anne Jasheway

Bedtime Stories for Dogs

Bedtime Stories for Cats

The Rules for Cats:
The Secret to Getting Free Catnip for Life

Give Me a Break:
For Women Who Have Too Much to Do!

The Rules for Dogs
The Secret to Getting Free Treats for Life

Leigh Anne Jasheway

Andrews and McMeel
A Universal Press Syndicate Company
Kansas City

Library of Congress Cataloging-in-Publication Data
Jasheway, Leigh Anne.
   The rules for dogs : the secret to getting free treats for life /
by Leigh Anne Jasheway.
      p.   cm.
ISBN 0-8362-3292-5 (pbk.)
1. Fein, Ellen. The rules—Parodies, imitations, etc. 2. Dogs—
Humor. 3. American wit and humor. I. Title
PN6231.P3J375   1997
818'.5407—dc21   96-51662
                                                                  CIP

This book is not associated with *The Rules* by Ellen Fein and Sherrie Schneider and is not published by the publisher of *The Rules*.

To Copper, Slate, and Maddy Lou, my dog children who always play with their food and never clean their rooms, but I don't care. And to the eight cats I grew up with who taught me how to scratch and claw until I got what I wanted. Finally, to Paul, my husband, the only human who'll put up with me.

Contents

The Rules for Dogs

The History of
The Rules for Dogs

$\mathbf{A}$ long time ago (especially if you count in dog years), my mother made me sit and stay. Then she said "Life is like a box of dog treats. Sometimes they have a meaty gravy coating and sometimes they do not." No, no. That's another book.

What Mom said in this case was "Lassie didn't get by on good looks alone, you know. She memorized The Rules for Dogs until she could bark them in her sleep. In fact, when everyone thought she was saying 'Timmy's stuck in the well,' what she really meant was 'Rule #17— Keep Your Leash On.'

"Anyway, as a result of abiding by the rules, she not only had all the rawhide bones she could chew, she had free-flowing mineral water in her toilet bowl."

So, like my mother and my grandmother before her (both of whom wore emerald-studded dog collars and never had to go outside to use the bushes in the rain), I have followed The Rules for Dogs to a *t*. Well, maybe to an *m*. I'm not sure because I'm not really very good at my alphabet. Hey, I'm a dog. What do you expect, a world-class speller?

But back to my point. As a result of The Rules for Dogs, I am lying here in my warm, comfy brass bed, snuggled under my handmade canine quilt, watching Eddie the Dog on *Frasier* while my people scurry around the house cleaning up my messes. And if I want, all I have to do is give *that look,* and my people will fetch me my slippers!

After years of sharing the rules with my friends Alex, Murray, and Tiny (you don't even want to know) at the fire hydrant, I decided it was only fair to write them down so that dogs everywhere could share in the good life. Well, actually, I didn't write the rules down. I had my people do it for me. It's true. If you don't believe me, I'll have my people call your people. They'll do that for me.

What Are The Rules for Dogs?

The purpose of The Rules for Dogs is to make your person as obsessed with you as you are with your hindquarters.

If you follow the rules, your person will start treating you like the king or queen that you are. They will sleep on the floor so you can have more room on the bed. They will order expensive trinkets from Nieman Barcus. They will take you on exotic vacations where you can scent-mark trees never before touched by doggie paws.

The most important thing about The Rules for Dogs is that you have to follow them all. You can't just follow a few of them and skip the rest. That would be like only making one and a half circles before you lie down. It just wouldn't work.

Meet a Rules Dog

You've probably met dozens, maybe even packs, of dogs just like Alex. She's not exceptionally good-looking or exceptionally bright. (Let's be honest, here. She still chases her own tail!) In fact, when you come right down to it, Alex is just your average, flea-bitten mangy mutt.

But unlike other AKC-registered dogs—dogs with names like Duke Westerbury The Third—who chase cars and come every time they hear their name or a whistle or even a can opener, Alex is selective.

She doesn't wag her tail at every Tom, Dick, and Rover. She only drools when it's really called for. And she would never go on David Letterman's Stupid Pet Tricks without a big cash advance up front.

Alex is a doggone good example of how far a dog can go if she follows The Rules for Dogs. After I shared The Rules with her one day out by our favorite bush, Alex immediately transformed herself. And as a result, her human eventually proposed moving to a log cabin in the woods. Now she has squirrels as far as the eye can see and a new tree to do her business on every time she goes out!

While other dogs are begging and whining and slobbering all over anyone who gives them a second glance, dogs like Alex sit and stay in the lap of luxury.

If you ask Alex what her secret is, she'll tell you. She'll tell you to quit jumping up on total strangers. She'll tell you to quit getting so excited you piddle on the floor whenever someone brings you a doggy bag. She'll insist that you turn your snout in the other direction whenever someone yells, "Fetch."

Now you may think that The Rules for Dogs violate every principle of dogdom. "Isn't dog supposed to be man's (or woman's) best friend?" you may be asking. Well, that's where you're mistaken. In the original Shitsu, the actual saying is "Man (or woman) is a dog's best friend when trained properly." As you can sniff, a lot was lost in the translation.

We all know dogs like Alex. They seem to be experts at getting what they want with a flick of their tail or a shake of their wet, loose skin on the morning newspaper. We can learn from them. This book will show you how.

Rule #1 _____

Be a Canine
Unlike Any Other

You don't have to be rich, beautiful, or even obedient to have the world at your paws. You simply have to have the right attitude. The attitude that says, "It doesn't matter that I have dog breath, drool incessantly, and have flea condos on my backside. I'm beautiful and I know it."

Once you've established this attitude, everything about you will attract attention—from the way you knock over important visitors when you greet them at the door to the way you clear a coffee table with one wag of your tail. You won't be able to enter a room without every person in it trying to get your dog-tag number.

If you have an attitude problem, you may need to enroll in Doggy Charm School (not to be confused with Obedience School), where they'll teach you poise, grace, and how to get your human to serve you kibble while balancing a book on his or her head and singing "The Rain in Spain Falls Mainly on the Plain." Sure, taking time out to go back to school will take time away from chasing flies and barking at shadows, but in the long run, it will be worth it.

You'll know when you've got the right attitude. You'll never be the whiner. You'll be the whinee. You'll never appear desperate, even if it's been weeks since someone has rubbed your belly and invited you out for rawhide bones and toilet water. You'll never settle, at least not for less than a nice velvet couch where you can stretch out your full length and get the full twenty-three hours of sleep you deserve.

If you follow Rule #1, you're well on your way to your just rewards. Sit back; relax. Your human is on the way to being trained!

Rule #2 _____

Don't Speak First

Wait patiently for people to speak to you. Sure they speak in gibberish that makes no sense to the intelligent canine, always harping on silly words like "stay" and "come," but you should just sit there with a patient and understanding look on your face. This pleases them and makes them think you've bonded.

If you find it too difficult to hold your tongue, get a nice muzzle.

Sometimes you may find that the person with whom you're trying to establish a relationship is just too shy to open up, so you may need to try one of these quick tips to get the ball rolling:

- Slobber lovingly on the rug.
- Make them jealous by wagging your tail shamelessly at everyone else in the room.
- Leave gifts all around the house, especially in dark places where they won't be discovered until later— like in shoes and behind the couch.
- Buy those little refrigerator magnets with words on them and spell out things like, "We need to talk."

Rule #3 _____

Never Ask a
Person to Dance

It's a matter of anatomy—they have two legs and you have four. Plus, they have no tail, so their sense of balance is not very well developed. As a result, you're going to have more natural dancing ability and rhythm. I mean, have you seen a person trying to do the Macarena?

If for some reason you come into a room and a person is attempting to dance, do not lie down on the floor and cover your eyes because this will humiliate and demean them. Instead, just pretend you see a fly and rush around the room madly until the dancing stops. Then, flop onto the couch and relax. You deserve it.

If your person ever brings up the subject of dancing, play dumb. It's in their best interest.

Rule #4 _____

Don't Let a Human Stare You Down

In a perfect world, no one—human or canine—would ever try to assert themselves as the dominant dog. Unfortunately, however, there are many misguided people who for some reason believe that they are in charge. Perhaps it is because they pay the mortgage or are putting you through Dog University.

One of the best ways to remind your human just exactly who runs things around the house is to stare him or her down. Follow these quick tips for best results:

1. Find a nice comfortable spot, such as on a beanbag chair or in the Bahamas. Have a seat.
2. Casually make eye contact.
3. Hold the stare for five to seven minutes.
4. Without looking away, walk toward the human and have a seat on his or her feet. This will cause them to loose all feeling in their toes within minutes.
5. While your human is up trying to get rid of foot cramps, triumphantly take over the entire sofa and nosh on the chips and dip.

Mission accomplished!

Rule #5 _____

Don't Go Dutch
on a Date

The Dutch may be geniuses at tulips, but they know absolutely nothing about fine dining. French, Italian, and even Chinese are preferred. Avoid lobster, however, because humans usually make a mess of it, leaving pieces scattered all over the place.

A few other simple rules about dining:

- Never inhale your food like a vacuum cleaner. Wait several minutes after the food has been delivered so that your person will think you couldn't care less. Then, quietly and elegantly nibble.
- Don't allow your ears to flop in your food. Try a nice diamond-encrusted barrette. If your ears do get inadvertently covered with Alpo, immediately dip them into the water dish and shake violently until all food particles are on the walls, not on the ears.

Never overturn the dish and scatter the contents all over the floor—unless, of course, your person has been seeing other dogs on the side.

Rule #6 _____

Don't Meet
Your Person Halfway

If you run to the door every time you need to go out, your person will feel that you are too independent and they might as well get a cat. So don't walk all the way over to the door and scratch. Simply raise an eyebrow in the general direction of your person. Believe me, they'll get the message. Try it now, I'll wait.

See?

Many humans will install a doggy door because they really believe it is more convenient for you. It's not—it's more convenient for them. Never, ever use a doggy door. It's beneath you. Just lie there on the couch until your human gets up and opens the door. Sure, it may seem like you're making them do a lot of work, but more than anything else, people want to know you need them. Let them know—over and over and over.

Rule #7 _____

Don't Call Out Your Person's Name in Your Sleep

We all have those dreams where we kick our hind legs and make little whimpering noises, and that's just fine. In fact, if you're dreaming about Rin Tin Tin or Fabio, it's even better than fine.

You don't, however, want your human to think that they are the person of your dreams. It's better if they think you have an active fantasy life in which they aren't included. This makes them even more desperate to love you the way you should be loved.

So before you go to bed each night, practice what you will say if you accidentally bark out in your sleep. (Something like, "Whoa, look at the size of that Great Dane!" will work just fine.)

Rule #8 _____

Don't Return
Your Person's Calls

If you come too easily every time your human calls, he or she will begin to think you have nothing better to do with your time. Make it clear that you live a busy life and have a lot of other friends—friends who appreciate your breath and the fact that you bring them slimy things from the yard.

If you're in the middle of urgent dog work, such as standing in the yard barking at changes in the barometric pressure, and your human comes to the door and hollers your name, it is nothing more than a cry for attention. If you immediately bound inside, your human will never learn to fend for himself or herself.

If instead you remain in the yard, sniffing out slugs and squirrels, the human will learn to appreciate the complexity of your life and the importance of your role in the universe. This will increase his or her respect for you, and the chances you'll get fed more than once a day will triple. This is a very good thing.

Rule #9 _____

Always End
Phone Calls

It is a proven fact that 93.7 percent of phone calls occur during your dinnertime. This can be very frustrating, not to mention how it can affect your blood sugar if you don't get your meals on time.

You have a number of options here. You can choose to bark incessantly the instant the phone rings and not stop until ten minutes after your human has hung up. This, however, can be taxing on your delicate voice.

A better choice is to bury the phone in the backyard whenever you have an opening in your schedule. In fact, this is so important, you should go ahead and pencil it on your calendar now.

Rule #10 _____

Don't Accept a Saturday Night Walk After 8:00 P.M.

It doesn't matter if your person did have a hot date. If you don't get your 7:00 P.M. walk, just use the hand-loomed Persian rug. You won't be taken for granted the next time.

There are other times when you should refuse a walk:

- When it's raining, snowing, sleeting, hailing, or just so darned sunny that you might get premature skin damage.
- Within one hour of having eaten a large meal (such as the Thanksgiving turkey that someone left for you on the middle of the dining room table).
- When your favorite TV shows, like *Scooby-Doo*, are on.
- When you're not done giving your human the cold shoulder for taking you to the vet.
- When you'd rather not.

Rule #11 _____

Fill Up Your Time Before Your Person Gets Home

If you spend your time waiting for your person all day, you'll get irritated and bored, and you'll have nothing to talk about. So make sure you occupy your time doing all the things that make you happy. Chase your tail, visit the Museum of Modern Fire Hydrants, go to an Ingmar Bir-dog retrospective, chew a nice pair of Ferragamo loafers and matching handbag . . . You'll both be happier in the long run. Shoeless, but happier.

Rule #12 _____

How to Act on
Dates 1, 2, and 3

When you and your human first meet, it can be nerve-wracking and piddle-inducing for you both. Here are some quick tips for making those first three dates come off without a hitch (or a leash):

- Until you know each other better, try to minimize your drooling. This is especially true if either of you is wearing silk.
- Speaking of silk, it is best to look good, but be careful not to overdress. Your basic black is always a surefire winner, as are classic sweaters in camel or tweed. Make sure to wear a clean dog collar every day. You wouldn't want to get in an accident with a ratty old dog collar on. If you are chubby, avoid horizontal stripes and matching knee socks.
- Don't drink from the toilet or roll on your back and expose your stomach on the first three dates.
- Don't whine about your last human all night long.

Rule #13 _____

How to Act on Dates 4 through When You're Sleeping on the Bed under the Covers

Once you've gotten the first three dates under your collar, you pretty much are free to be yourself, although you may want to hold off licking your private parts and perfuming the air with your natural odors until date 417 or so.

Another important rule for those later dates has to do with flirting. Basically, you shouldn't flirt with others while on a date. In particular, don't flirt with inanimate objects. This makes humans very uncomfortable. Especially out in public.

If you are trying to begin a long-term relationship with a human, brushing up against another human is okay, but keep your nose to yourself. Quick tip: If you find yourself about to remove your dog collar, the flirting has gone too far. A nice cold shower should help. Be sure to shake off right next to your intended so that he or she knows just how much you are giving up for this relationship.

Rule #14 _____

Stop Seeing Your Person If He or She Doesn't Buy You a Romantic Gift for Your Birthday or Valentine's Day

A new self-feeding dog dish or pooper scooper just doesn't make the cut. Hold out for a bouquet of rawhide roses or a black lace leash and harness.

On the other hand, as a general rule of thumb, you are not expected to get a gift for your person unless he or she really deserves it. If you do choose to leave a gift, remember, always top it off with a bow.

Don't Let Them See You in the Garbage More Than Once or Twice a Week

Now you know and I know that rooting through the garbage is one of life's simple pleasures. Unfortunately, most humans don't appreciate the fine art of ripping apart a nice paper bag and strewing its rotting contents all over the linoleum.

Besides, some things should be just your little pleasures. They are not meant to be shared. So only get into the trash when your human is out. And when they come home and ask you if you did it, smile innocently and lick that last bit of peanut butter off your snout.

Rule #16 _____

No More Than Casual Kissing on the First Date

You may find this hard to believe, but most humans don't want you to kiss them on the mouth. They're just inhibited, that's all.

It is best to wait until the second date before planting a nice, sloppy kiss on your person's lips. Often you will have to do this when they are not paying attention, such as when they're watching *Melrose Place* or sleeping on the couch (or watching *Melrose Place* while sleeping on the couch). Another good ploy is to pretend to be looking in one direction and then swing around the other way and plant a big, wet one right on their lips. Then, go back to licking yourself.

Rule #17 _____

Keep Your Leash On and Other Rules for Intimacy

Yes, it's true that a leash can get sweaty and annoying, especially in the heat of, well, the day. But you must never let your human pressure you into removing your leash until you are good and ready.

And before you remove your leash under any circumstances, ask yourself, "Will my person still respect me in the morning? And will they take me for a jog even if they're late for a busy meeting?"

You may want to practice removing your leash in private so that you can do it gracefully. There's nothing worse than getting that buckle caught on your dog tag when you're trying to look seductive.

Rule #18 _____

Don't Let Them
Tell You to Sit

Humans seem to be fascinated with sitting. They do it all the time and for some reason, they think you should too.

But you're a busy canine. You've got e-mail to send to the SPCA. You've got shoes to examine. You've got imaginary burglars to intimidate. Sitting is just not something you can fit in right now.

So the next time your human tells you to "sit," simply stare with that vacant look that we all know so well—the one that says, "You know, I'd really like to help you out, here, but I don't speak your language. Perhaps if you went back to school and became bilingual we could discuss this at a later time."

Or you could just wander off and roll in something smelly in the yard. Your choice.

Rule #19 _____

Let Your Person Take the Lead

Sure it would be nice to be the lead dog for a change, but if you're in this relationship for the long haul, you must make your human believe he or she is in control.

Fortunately, it is not difficult to fool humans. If you keep your eyes lowered and pretend to be listening to what they say, you can train them to do almost anything you'd like. You might start with such tricks as:

- The "Move Over, I Need That Part of the Couch" Trick
- The "You Forgot to Feed Me Again" Trick (Depending upon your human's memory, you may be able to play this trick eight or nine times in one day.)
- The "Go to the Door, There's Someone There!" Trick (This is especially fun to do in the middle of the night when your human is sound asleep.)
- The "Isn't This Mud I Tracked in Making a Nice Design on the Carpet?" Trick

Remember, however, that you don't want to flaunt your intellectual superiority by making your human perform stupid tricks too often. Just once in a while when you feel the need to amuse yourself. And don't forget: Always let them think they're the boss.

Rule #20 _____

Never Let Them See You Pant

It doesn't matter how hot you get, once you start to pant, you'll never recover that aura of cool composure you've worked so long to maintain. Before you meet your person, you may want to take a nice, cool shower. Lather up with a gentle flea shampoo, and you'll kill two birds, uh, fleas, with one stone, so to speak.

As a general rule, you should avoid panting altogether. However, if you absolutely must, you may pant in the following situations:

- aerobics or clog dancing
- while being interrogated for a crime
- during Arnold Schwarzenegger movies
- while modeling the latest canine fashions under bright lights

Rule #21 _____

Practice Safe Riding

No matter how eager you are, never get in the car unless your person has buckled up and made sure that the canine air bag is fully functional. You may also want to check his or her breath for signs of alcohol or dog treats.

Once inside the car, you should always:

- Avoid standing on the driver's lap as this could cause him or her to swerve into traffic and thus shorten your ride.
- Alternate sides of the car so that your ears remain symmetrical.
- Only ride inside. Dogs who ride in the back of pickups are, well, neanderdogs.
- Do not attempt to leave the vehicle while it is moving, even if you see a squirrel so slow you're sure you could catch it.
- Never ride in a Yugo. Word gets out.

Rule #22 _____

If It Itches,
Don't Scratch It

Scratching yourself in public, especially in those certain areas of the body, you know the ones I mean, is gauche and lower class. You spend two or three hours gnawing at your private parts trying to get relief, and you may find yourself out on the street looking for a new home.

To avoid this situation, never, ever scratch:

- at the opera (even while the fat lady is singing)
- in a limo (unless it's a stretch and absolutely no one will see or hear you)
- while accepting an Oscar
- under a sunbrella on the Riviera
- while having your portrait painted
- during a seven-course meal at Buckingham Palace
- on the veranda sipping mint juleps through a rawhide chew toy

If you find yourself in any of these situations and an uncontrollable itch occurs, your best bet is to find a nice, out-of-the-way place, such as a large woman's skirt or under the table. There, in the privacy of your hiding spot, you can scratch away to your heart's content.

Rule #23 _____

No Matter How Desperate You Are, Don't Beg

Begging makes you appear needy and pathetic. Instead, go for the direct approach—a cold nose against any warm part of the human anatomy usually gets immediate attention.

Rule #24 _____

Don't Sleep with a Person Until the Time Is Right

This rule is easy to follow since sleeping occupies nine-tenths of a dog's time. Therefore, the rule is that the time is always right. It is still always good advice to never jump into someone's bed the first time you meet them. If you wake up and the person sharing your pillow calls you "Rover" or "Fido" when your dog tag clearly says "Fifi," you've made a serious relationship error.

When you do decide to share a person's bed, make sure to sprawl out across the bed to take up as much space as you can. This makes your human feel safe and secure. Regular kicking during the night will remind him or her that you could use a nice drink of water if they happen to be getting up.

Sleeping etiquette is important to humans. It's good advice to try not to fall asleep while your human is talking to you. This is seen as rude. As soon as the human pauses to take a breath, however, you are free to doze off.

Other tips about sharing a bed:

- When you have one of those dreams (you know the ones I mean), go ahead and yip and kick your back legs and get that crazy smile on your face. Your human lives vicariously through you, and this is the most excitement he or she has in life.

- If you have difficulty falling asleep, make sure everyone else is up too. You can discuss the relationship or have a late-night snack together.
- When snoozing during the day, be sure to claim the only available patch of sunlight or the spot in front of the heater. After all, you've had a long, hard day barking, protecting the house from imaginary intruders, and you need your rest.

Rule #25 _____

Don't Expect a Human to Change

Let's say your human has a nasty little habit, like always forgetting to heat your dinner up in the microwave before putting it in your dish or always putting the toilet lid down. You may want to believe that somehow you can change him or her and that in a couple of weeks things will be going just like you want. Wrong.

Due to their inferior brain capacity, humans are only capable of changing three things—their minds, their underwear, and lanes on the freeway. If you are generally unhappy about the direction a relationship is going, it is better to get out in the early stages—before you've invested too much time and tail-wagging.

There is one method, however, that while not solving your problem permanently may give you a temporary solution to dealing with your human's bad habits. As soon as he or she has fallen asleep, begin a low, steady howl—a howl so intense coyotes in the desert sit up and howl back. A howl so ear-splitting, even deafened old rock 'n' rollers can hear it.

If you do this every night for three or four weeks, you may see some slight changes in your human's behavior. But don't get your hopes up.

Rule #26 _____

Don't Live with a Middle-Aged Woman with Cats

Anyone who owns cats is mentally unstable. A middle-aged woman with more than one cat will probably end up in the local loony bin. And how will she feed you from there? Not to mention the fact that cats are always going around with that superior-than-thou attitude, even when they have kitty litter stuck to the bottoms of their feet.

Rule #27 _____

Don't Date
a Married Human

Many people who are married have the crazy idea that they should place the needs of their spouse before your needs. Now you know this is ludicrous and illogical. I mean, have you ever seen a spouse fetch slippers or catch a Frisbee in his or her mouth? What can I say, humans are stupid that way.

What you need is a nice, single person—preferably a divorced, forty-something woman who works at home and has no hobbies or friends. This will give her plenty of time to attend to your needs. You may, however, want to avoid menopausal women. They're always fiddling with the thermostat, not to mention the fact they occasionally vacuum in the nude because of hot flashes.

You should also never date people with small children or a rap sheet.

Rule #28 _____

Keep Them Away
from Your Family

You don't want to rush your human into meeting your family. Especially if your family is dysfunctional. You know the type—addicted to toilet water, never practicing birth control, involved with the mailman . . . Besides, do you really want your human to find out you were the runt of the litter?

Save yourself the grief and avoid introducing your human to your canine family. It'll save you years in pet therapy.

Now, you may find that your human really wants to meet your family. Especially if a holiday is right around the corner—a holiday like Thanksgiving or Christmas or The Time of the Great Butt-Sniffing.

Do anything you can to wheedle out of this meeting. You might try:

- peeing on the tires
- hiding the car keys under the sofa
- developing a slight limp and a pitiful look (Don't go too far with this one. You want your human to feel sorry for you and stay home with you. You do not want to end up at the vet's.)
- hissing (Hey, it works for cats!)

Rule #29 _____

Follow the Rules for Dogs Even When Your Friends Think It's Nuts

Your friends don't really have a clue about what it takes to wrap a human around their paw. So why should you listen to them? In fact, why are they even your friends? When it comes right down to it, they're nothing but a bunch of mixed breeds with no manners and poor housebreaking.

Take my advice—get better friends. No, not the ones on TV who sit around all day drinking cappuccino. (Who in their right mind would drink that stuff when there's a nice toilet right next door?) Find dogs who can live up to your demanding, but in no way unreasonable, expectations.

Rule #30 _____

Rules for
Obedience School

Now you know and I know that you're much too smart to hang out with the social rejects who show up in obedience school. If you're going to school, it should be a private college, with nice doggy dorms and fire hydrants in every class.

Why waste your time learning inane commands like "roll over" and "down" when you could be studying the great minds of history like Dogcrates and Caninestein?

Rule #31 _____

Don't Discuss The Rules with Your Therapist or Your Veterinarian

Your therapist is paid to think that you are imbalanced and your veterinarian is paid to stick things, well, you know where. Why would you bother to talk to them about anything? Especially if you're paying for the time?

Take my advice and only share The Rules for Dogs with your other worthy canine friends.

Rule #32 _____

Be Easy to
Live With

Once your relationship with a human is solid—you're sharing a couch, a bed, and a toothbrush—you should concentrate on being as easy to get along with as possible.

Here are some tips:

- Don't bare your teeth unless it is absolutely necessary, such as when there is a burglar on *America's Most Wanted,* a meter reader is within a ten-mile radius of the house, your water dish is empty, you're bored, there's nothing good on TV, or the dog biscuits are stale.
- Don't invite friends over from the pound without asking first.
- Don't whine all the time. Your human will think you're a nag. Try a little variety—whining, whimpering, hounding, barking, howling, etc.
- Never threaten to go home to mother every time any little thing goes wrong around the house. This tactic never works because your human gets all excited about the prospect of getting to work the remote control for a change.

Last, but Not Least, 12 Extra Hints

1. When your human asks you to come out from under the comforter, silently count to five hundred thousand. It will make him or her all the more appreciative of your presence.
2. Do the absolute minimum. Always. Try to do even less.
3. When you're invited out to a cat show and you'd rather go galloping through a nice mud puddle, plop your butt down on the linoleum and refuse to budge.
4. When walking down the street, drop hints, ever so slightly, that you'd like to be carried.
5. Be affectionate. Look at yourself in the mirror and tell yourself what a stunning creature you are.
6. If your human is misbehaving, taking you for granted, or treating you like a cat, remember the howl-long-and-loud-until-things-change trick. It works just as well here. Then quietly sit nearby with an innocent look on your face, as if to say, "Did I wake you?"
7. If you are unsure as to whether this is going to work into a long-term commitment, move on with your life. There are plenty of biscuits in the box: —beef, chicken, lamb, and rice. . . .

8. Occasionally, your human will say things to irk you such as, "Tomorrow we'll go in to get you fixed." Don't get mad; get the scissors.

9. Don't let him or her know that you're afraid to be home alone without a can opener.

10. Don't get angry if your human takes longer to change your flea collar than you would like. If you're following The Rules For Dogs it will get done! If not, a nice present in your human's briefcase will usually do the trick.

11. Don't let your humans get sloppy with their looks. Make sure they get their daily exercise by waiting on you hand and foot.

12. Lie on the newspaper so your human pays attention to you, not to a bunch of stupid stories that don't have anything to do with you.

Well, those are The Rules for Dogs. Once you've finished this book, please pass it along to canine friends. But ask them not to dog-ear the corners. That's just plain rude.

The Rules-at-a-Glance

Rule 1   Be a Canine Unlike Any Other

Rule 2   Don't Speak First

Rule 3   Never Ask a Person to Dance

Rule 4   Don't Let a Human Stare
You Down

Rule 5   Don't Go Dutch on a Date

Rule 6   Don't Meet Your Person Halfway

Rule 7   Don't Call Out Your Person's Name
in Your Sleep

Rule 8   Don't Return Your Person's Calls

Rule 9   Always End Phone Calls

Rule 10 Don't Accept a Saturday Night Walk
After 8:00 P.M.

Rule 11 Fill Up Your Time Before Your
Person Gets Home

Rule 12 How to Act on Dates 1, 2, and 3

Rule 13 How to Act on Dates 4 through
When You're Sleeping on the Bed
under the Covers

Rule 14 Stop Seeing Your Person If He or
She Doesn't Buy You a Romantic
Gift for Your Birthday or Valentine's
Day

Rule 15 Don't Let Them See You in the
Garbage More Than Once or Twice
a Week

Rule 16 No More Than Casual Kissing on
the First Date

About the Author

Leigh Anne Jasheway is a comedy writer and stand-up comic who lives in Eugene, Oregon, with her three giant wiener dogs, her much younger spouse (who is regularly mistaken for a high schooler), and lots of dust. Her hobbies include photography, frisbee golf, and lifting short-legged dogs onto the couch. In her next life, she wants her own bed.